Betrayed Valor

A Veteran's Story of Service, Sacrifice, and Systemic Neglect

by Dr. Sammie L. Young

Publisher:
Betrayed Valor Publishing — Dr. Sammie Young

For inquiries & media contact:
TikTok: @betrayedvalorchief_young
Facebook: @BetrayedValorVeterans Speak Out
Instagram: @dr.sammieyoung

ISBNs:
Paperback ISBN: 979-8-9940679-1-8
Hardcover ISBN: 979-8-9940679-3-2
E-book ISBN: 979-8-9940679-0-1
Audiobook ISBN: 979-8-9940679-2-5

Library of Congress Control Number: Pending
Printed in the United States of America

This work is a truthful account based on lived experiences. Some dialogue and events may be recreated for clarity while preserving historical accuracy and integrity.

Dedicated to every veteran, service member, and public servant who stood their post with honor — and to those still fighting their battles long after service ends. You are not forgotten.

DEDICATION

For my late wife,
Denise Floretta "Neecee Baby" Young (RIP) —
you walked beside me through the darkest valleys
and never once let go of my hand.
Even in your final days,
you held our family together with quiet strength.
Your love outlived your time on earth,
and I carry it with me still.

To our children — Omar, Sammie Jr., and Lamar —
and our grandchildren — Lashun, Tresean, Lamarion, and
Trinity this book stands as proof that even when life breaks
you down, love can still carry you forward. Your
grandmother's voice lives in every word.

IN HONOR OF

My Aunt — Betty Morgan

The oldest living member of our family and one of the strongest women I know. You carry the wisdom of those who came before us, and you kept our family history alive when others might have forgotten it. Your stories kept my roots strong, and your belief in me gave me courage when I had none left.

Thank you for being our bridge to the past — and for helping me walk toward the future.

ACKNOWLEDGMENTS

I want to thank the colleagues who stood by me during the hardest parts of this journey. I may not list every name here, but you know who you are. Your support — whether spoken out loud or shown quietly — meant more than I can explain.

Some of you were witnesses to what I endured, and others offered strength when I had very little left. Your encouragement reminded me that even in struggle, there are people who still care — people who choose to stand on the side of what's right.

To each person who checked in, listened, or believed in me when it counted most — thank you. Your presence helped me reach this moment, and I will always remember it.

SPECIAL THANKS — BOOK COVER DESIGN

I want to give a special thanks to someone whose creativity made a strong impact on this book. The front and back cover were both designed by Kayla M. Gilmore of KMG Creations Productions, and her work speaks for itself. She didn't just create a cover — she captured the spirit of this book with excellence and respect, and I want to recognize that openly.

"Kayla M. Gilmore is the visionary behind Starkville, Mississippi's first Veterans Day Parade, launched in 2018 and still held annually. Her advocacy began in 2009 and beyond with annual Veterans dance celebrations, leading her to raise the bar in 2018 by organizing the city's first official parade. She is widely respected for her dedication and commitment to honoring those who served."

For anyone looking to collaborate or inquire about professional cover design, here is her information:

Front and back cover designed by:
Kayla M. Gilmore — KMG Creations Productions
Website:
Email: kmgcreationsproductions@gmail.com

Kayla — you earned this recognition. With respect.

Table of Contents

SYSTEM DENIAL TIMELINE — FACTUAL SUMMARY

A condensed factual list of denials, requests, and decisions — based on official records.

This section outlines where the system failed to follow procedure, offer accommodation, or provide due process.

1. Reasonable Accommodation Request — Mishandled

I requested reasonable accommodation due to health limitations.

The VA never provided an interactive process, as required by federal law.

I was removed without ever being placed on a Performance Improvement Plan (PIP).

I was later removed — instead of being reassigned, accommodated, or protected.

2. CRSC (Combat-Related Special Compensation) Denial

I qualified under multiple combat-related factors — including operational deployments and a VA disability rating.

My CRSC application was denied without evaluating supporting evidence. I literally commanded LCU-1666 in time of War.

The appeal was delayed and mishandled.

DoD is supposed to adopt VA service-connected decisions
— but did not in my case.

3. COVID Remote Request

I was initially denied until I submitted for higher level
review.

No alternative duties were offered.

Leadership stated I had to be physically present to perform
my job — but this directly contradicted CDC guidance for
individuals with qualifying medical conditions.

4. Forced Removal & Lack of Due Process

I was removed without being offered:

Opportunity to defend the false counseling which was one
of the elements used for removal

Modified duties, instead further training denied. The trainer
was instructed not to continue training me. Additionally,
my access was pulled, so I was unable to work.

Transfer opportunities despite legal request

5. Disparate Treatment & Inconsistent Standards

Other employees were reassigned, promoted, or retained.

I was denied every opportunity for relief.

This shows inconsistent treatment — contradicting fair
employment practice.

6. Outcomes Still in Motion

CRSC denial still under review

Accommodation-related removal is part of MSPB
proceedings

I do not seek sympathy — only accountability

This timeline is based on official submissions, emails,
medical records, and agency responses. It is included not to
accuse — but to document. History deserves a record.

Chapter 1 – The Making of a Leader

Betrayed Valor: A Veteran's Story of Service, Sacrifice, and Systemic Neglect

by Dr. Sammie Young

My name is Sammie Young, and I was born in Columbus, Mississippi. My mother, Mildred Jean Young, deserves to have her name spoken first, because everything I am came from her. She was a single mother raising seven children—three sons and four daughters—while battling diabetes, high blood pressure, and arthritis. She taught us the meaning of work, faith, and responsibility. When my older brothers left home, I became the one who helped her keep the household together. In today's world people might call that "parentification," but back then it was simply what a son did. I became the disciplinarian, the stabilizer, the one who made sure the family stayed in line.

Leadership found me early. On the football field I weighed barely 120 pounds, yet I played defensive end and offensive guard. Those were the toughest positions, but toughness never scared me. It built in me what I call the warrior instinct—that refusal to quit no matter the odds.

That same instinct carried me into the United States Navy. I didn't enlist to escape trouble; I enlisted to seek purpose. I joined through the Delayed Entry Program, already dreaming of oceans bigger than anything I had seen in Mississippi. From the moment I stepped into boot camp I was chosen as a squad leader, guiding other recruits through the chaos of early military life.

My first ship assignment confirmed what my mother already knew: leadership was in my blood. I advanced quickly—frocked to E-4, then made E-5—and earned the trust of my chain of command. As a Training Petty Officer, I was responsible for qualifying and shaping other sailors. I completed my Enlisted Surface Warfare Specialist (ESWS) qualification as an E-5, something usually reserved for senior petty officers. I attacked every PQS (Personal Qualification Standard) I could find, because knowledge was how you served your crew.

The Navy kept putting me in places where leadership mattered most. I became a Company Commander—what other branches call a drill instructor—and at only twenty-two years old I was leading men sometimes older than me. Every company I trained earned full colors and top honors. Out of hundreds of instructors I ranked in the top ten percent and was rewarded with a follow-on duty station in Mobile, Alabama.

From there I served as Leading Petty Officer aboard the USS Jesse L. Brown, a reserve frigate we were preparing to transfer to the Egyptian Navy. Later came the USS Cleveland LPD-7, where I served as Drug and Alcohol Program Advisor (DAPA) to the commanding officer—a job that demanded judgment, empathy, and absolute integrity. I also attended Recruiter School, Naval Leadership School in Coronado, and taught leadership to officers and enlisted personnel alike. Some of those young leaders I taught have probably gone on to become senior officers, maybe even senators. I taught them what my mother taught me: listen, lead, and do right when nobody's watching.

The proudest billet of my career was serving as Craft Master of a 165-foot amphibious assault craft—an LCU. You didn't get that job by seniority; you earned it through skill, judgment, and grit. The evaluator said mine was "the best qualification package ever submitted." I ran flawless drills—no man-overboard incidents, no safety violations—and soon we were called to war.

When the Iraq War began, my craft was part of the Marine Expeditionary Unit (16th MEU) delivering troops and equipment into Kuwait and onward to Baghdad. We transported over five million pounds of munitions, howitzers, tanks, and vehicles—everything the Marines needed to bring down Saddam Hussein. We literally drove into the belly of larger ships, rode the flood tide, and delivered freedom to the shore. For a kid from Mississippi, that was the pinnacle of service.

Out at sea I suffered a serious accident—the kind that changes your life forever. I earned a service-connected disability, though speaking about it sometimes brings new targets on your back. Still, I have no regrets. I served my country with distinction, dignity, and honor.

That experience taught me that serving doesn't end when the uniform comes off. It continues in how you live, how you fight for fairness, and how you stand for those who can't. This book is my attempt to do exactly that—to seek justice, not vengeance; to show how systems meant to protect veterans can instead break them; and to remind readers that the American Dream should never require you to lose everything twice.

I went from poverty to living the white-picket-fence dream—and back again. Yet I'm still here, still standing, still serving. Because as long as I have God, there will always be an up after every down.

The photograph that appears on the cover of this book was taken the day I received my shadow box—the traditional symbol of a sailor's service coming full circle. At the time I had no idea that moment would later mirror my life. In the picture, I stand in uniform, proud yet pensive, unaware that I would one day have to look inward and backward to understand what was coming. What I see in that image now is both the man I was and the man I had to become. It reminds me that reflection isn't just about the past; it's about recognizing the battles we carry forward.

That photo became more than a keepsake—it became a prophecy. It captured the moment before everything changed, the last instant of peace before the storm. And in it I still see strength, purpose, and the quiet faith that whatever comes next, I will endure.

Chapter 2 – Broken Promises

When I first got out of the military, it was hard for me to get a job. I had a master's degree at the time, and I was already building toward my doctorate in computer science. I thought those credentials, combined with my years of service and leadership, would make me an ideal candidate in the civilian world. I believed that being a veteran meant I would be supported in my transition. I assumed there would be a structured process, some sort of bridge from military service to meaningful civilian employment. But that bridge didn't exist—or if it did, I never found it.

I went out to the unemployment office, filled out applications, sent resumes, and sat through conversations that felt hollow. Being a veteran, I thought I would receive some kind of preferential treatment or, at the very least, a sense of urgency from the system designed to help me find a job. But instead, I found disappointment. There was no transitional space, no guided path, no counselor who really understood what it meant to start over after years of command and service. I stayed unemployed for nearly a year.

Finally, I got a call from Columbus Air Force Base. They needed an executive assistant—a personal assistant of sorts—to help manage the administrative side of operations. I was in charge of ensuring that the pilots being trained had housing, that their needs were met, and that their transitions were smooth. The Iraq War was still raging, so in my own way, I was still supporting the mission. I was helping the men and women who were about to carry the burden of combat. It gave me a renewed sense of purpose.

Still, it was a difficult adjustment. Going from being a senior leader—someone with authority and respect—to starting over in a civilian job wasn't easy. I had risen through the ranks in the Navy to Chief Petty Officer. I was used to leading, mentoring, and being relied upon. Now, I was just another employee. The civilian workplace was different. The camaraderie and esprit de corps that defined the military were missing. People worked in isolation. There wasn't the same sense of mission or unity of purpose. That was something I didn't realize I would miss so deeply.

I remember being told by someone at the unemployment office, "Well, this is a college town, so jobs might be hard to come by." That statement cut deep. It wasn't just the words—it was the lack of empathy, the casual dismissal of a veteran trying to find his place in the world again. It was unnerving to realize that after all the years of service, the system wasn't designed to catch you when you fell—it just watched you fall.

Eventually, I found stability at Columbus Air Force Base. There, I rediscovered some of what I had lost—the discipline, the purpose, the mission. I was surrounded by military professionals who spoke the same language I did. For a while, it felt like home again.

Then came the opportunity that would change everything: a position with the Department of Veterans Affairs. This was it. This was the dream job. I thought, "What better way to continue serving than to serve those who had already served?" The mission was clear. The purpose was noble. I was stepping into something that felt bigger than myself again.

When I started at the VA, I felt empowered. I believed in what the organization stood for. I was part of a team dedicated to helping veterans get the care they deserved. My role in information technology meant I was supporting that mission behind the scenes—keeping systems running, ensuring that the technology worked so that doctors and nurses could do their jobs. Veterans' health depended on it, and that responsibility meant something to me. It was my new form of service.

I started at a GS-5 level, earning around $50,000 a year. By 2007 or 2008, I had moved into the VA and my pay doubled. I worked hard for every advancement. I eventually reached GS-12 after years of dedication. I built my career step by step, applying for every opportunity, But not without challenges as my book will detail and proving my value over and over. It was the military mindset—work hard, earn respect, climb the ladder. And for a time, it worked.

Even with the long commute—an hour and a half each way—I was proud to do it. I was building something meaningful. I truly believed I had found the place where I could retire, contribute, and continue living the values I had learned in uniform. Everything was good as gold.

But I didn't anticipate what was coming next. The challenges that waited for me inside those walls were nothing like what I had faced in the Navy. In the military, your word meant something. In this new world, it was all about who you knew, not what you did. And I was about to learn that lesson the hard way.

Chapter 3 – The Inner Circle

You could always tell who belonged to the inner circle. They didn't walk the halls like the rest of us—they glided in formation. If you saw Bryant Lewis, you saw Calvin Williams and James Ray flanking him, moving as one. It wasn't just proximity; it was permission. They had access that didn't need to be announced. They had his ear before a decision, during a decision, and after it. And the rest of us learned those decisions the hard way—when the consequences landed on our desks.

On paper I was the senior technician—the person people came to when things broke and when the work nobody wanted had to get done. I didn't ask for favors, I delivered results. But results didn't matter as much in that office as relationships did. Calvin made sure the day began with Bryant's breakfast and ended with laughter in his doorway. James hovered in every conversation that mattered. If I offered a solution in a meeting, it was dismissed. If one of them repeated the same solution an hour later, it became the plan.

I don't mind earning respect. I've earned everything I have. But I do mind when the rules change depending on who's asking. That's what favoritism does—it rewrites the standards in pencil. The rest of us were graded in ink.

Take the morning rituals. Calvin sprinting out to buy breakfast wasn't about food; it was about signaling loyalty. Those small acts accumulated into large exemptions— flexibility on hours, grace on deadlines, and protection when work went sideways. For the rest of us, it was the opposite: heavier scrutiny, thinner patience, and no cover.

People noticed. They didn't always speak up, but they noticed. I wasn't looking for praise, but I was looking for fairness. Instead, I learned to keep my head down and let the output speak. Even then, the quiet work was easy to ignore. The laughs in the hallway were louder.

When Andrea Marshall arrived, the message became crystal clear. As lead tech, I should have been her mentor. I should have set her daily tasks, trained her, and evaluated her progress. I wasn't even told she'd been hired. One day she was simply there—walking the halls with Calvin as if she'd always belonged to the club. When I introduced myself and offered help, she barely made eye contact. It wasn't hostility; it was indoctrination. She had already been told the story of who to trust and who to avoid.

That's what the clique excelled at: narrative control. The 'who' mattered more than the 'what.' Talent wasn't cultivated, it was curated—selected for obedience and proximity. People who challenged decisions were framed as problems to be managed rather than professionals to be heard.

It was the little erasures that wore on me. I'd propose a fix on Monday, and by Wednesday it reappeared as someone else's idea. I didn't need my name on it; the veterans just needed working systems. But when leadership gets used to taking credit for quiet labor, they grow reliant on the quiet. They punish the voice that tries to correct the record.

Leon Layton saw it. He was a programmer and a straight shooter—old-school professional and retired Air Force E-8. He did the work thoroughly, told the truth plainly, and expected the same in return. In an office built on appearances, that made him dangerous. He watched the upstairs crew wander in late, lock their doors an hour before quitting time, and still collect the praise. He reported what he saw. Nothing changed—except the target on his back grew larger.

The clique didn't just create favorites; it created enemies. Not because we were rivals, but because we were reminders—proof that the mission could be accomplished without performance theater. That's the thing about cliques: they are allergic to accountability. They call neutrality 'disloyalty' and competence 'threatening.'

Bryant's comments gave away more than he realized. When a coworker casually mentioned we were from the same county and that I held a doctorate, Bryant snapped back that he would earn his degree from an accredited university—as if my achievements diminished him. That kind of insecurity in a leader calcifies into policy. It trickles down into who is trusted, who is promoted, and who gets punished for speaking plainly.

I kept my focus on the mission. I came to the VA to serve veterans—period. Keep the network stable. Keep the machines patched. Keep clinicians connected to care. That's what mattered. So I took on the ugly jobs, the ones that needed both expertise and humility. If something was broken long enough that everyone had given up on it, it would end up on my desk. And I welcomed the challenge.

But in a culture built on proximity, results become inconvenient facts. If success doesn't come from the right corner of the office, leadership struggles to celebrate it. Sometimes they ignore it; sometimes they repurpose it; sometimes they try to fail you on purpose so success never arrives at all. That last tactic became their favorite.

What I didn't know then—but learned soon enough—was how far the inner circle would go to preserve itself. It wasn't just about praise or positions. It was about control. If they couldn't shape the outcome, they would shape the narrative around the outcome. If they couldn't own the win, they would redefine the rules so the win didn't count.

I wish this chapter ended with a simple disagreement over style. It didn't. It escalated—into manipulated postings, staged failures, and fact-findings that were more theater than truth-seeking. The clique closed ranks, and the mission was pushed to the margins. And yet, even then, many of us kept doing the quiet work because we signed up to serve veterans, not egos.

What began as a pattern of breakfast meetings and closed doors became the engine for everything that followed. Promotions weren't just delayed; they were engineered. Projects weren't just difficult; they were booby-trapped. The next chapters show how the inner circle's preferences turned into policy—and how those policies were used to try to break me.

Chapter 4 – The Promotion Trap

Author's Note

There are moments in every journey where a person must decide whether to surrender to the weight of injustice or rise above it. For me, the choice was never surrender. Even when favoritism and systemic bias clouded the path forward, I believed that faith, integrity, and persistence would prevail. This chapter reflects not only what was taken from me but also what I refused to let die—my belief in purpose, in accountability, and in the power of standing firm for what's right.

When I look back on my federal career, 'The Promotion Trap' defines a painful truth: that merit alone was never enough. I earned my place through performance, education, and years of proven leadership. Yet again and again, I watched others—less qualified, often connected through favoritism—rise overnight while I was told to 'wait my turn.'

It started when the GS-12 positions were first announced. I met every qualification—time in grade, performance, leadership—everything that should have made me the natural candidate. The posting was internal, limited only to VA IT personnel, which meant there were no outside applicants to compete with. I interviewed alongside Tameka Mason and James Ray. I remember being confident because the work spoke for itself. My record was solid, my evaluations strong, and I had been performing duties well above my grade. But after the interviews, they pulled the job completely. They didn't cancel all openings—just mine. I knew then what time it was. It was never about merit. It was about control.

They reposted one of the two GS-12s later, but when they realized I was the only person with the required time and grade, they pulled it again. That's when I understood: they were never going to let me have that role because it was supposed to go to someone else—someone hand-picked. And sure enough, overnight, others like Calvin Williams and James Ray were rewarded while I was sidelined. I had done the work, trained others, led projects, and delivered beyond expectations. Yet, in the culture under Bryant Lewis's leadership, loyalty to him was the true currency, not performance.

I didn't stop there. I pushed for accountability and continued to perform. I took on massive workloads—like overseeing the Windows 10 to 11 upgrade project. That was no small feat. I set up imaging stations, sometimes producing twenty computers a day to meet deployment goals. No one else was doing that volume. I worked tirelessly, often staying late, just to keep the mission moving. I wasn't just doing my job—I was keeping the entire operation running. People would come by my office and ask, 'Sam, how are you doing all this?' And I'd just smile, because the truth was, I didn't have a choice. Failure wasn't an option for me.

But when Charles, one of my coworkers, took the very network switch I was using to stage those computers, my productivity dropped. When I questioned him, he dismissed me outright. I appealed to Lewis, but instead of support, I got suspicion. I moved my operations to a storage closet to keep things going, using my own initiative to get the job done. Lewis found out and used it against me—sent out an email in bold red letters threatening punishment for whoever placed computers in the closets. He already knew it was me. In the next meeting, he pretended ignorance, asking, 'Who did this?' I raised my hand. I wasn't going to lie. I explained the reason and reminded him that it was all

for the sake of meeting the mission. But my honesty
became another weapon against me.

He ordered a fact-finding investigation. I later learned he
asked someone outside our chain to handle it—someone he
knew would deliver the result he wanted. The findings came
back 'unfounded,' but that didn't stop him. The goal was
never justice; it was to document a trail, to paint me as a
problem. Over time, this became a pattern. Any initiative I
took, any success I had, would be repackaged under
someone else's name or buried entirely. Still, I refused to
quit. I believed the truth would stand on its own.

What hurt most wasn't just being passed over—it was
watching the integrity of the workplace decay. People who
once respected me began avoiding me out of fear of
retaliation from Lewis. Others aligned with him for safety or
opportunity. Andrea Marshall was one of those cases. She
was hired without my knowledge even though, as lead tech,
I should've been part of the onboarding. She had little IT
experience, but Lewis treated her like a protégé. Calvin took
her under his wing, walking her around like a trophy. I
didn't mind mentoring her, but she avoided me entirely. It
was clear Lewis had already poisoned her view of me.

Favoritism spread like a disease. Promotions were decided
over breakfast, not in performance reviews. Leon Layton, a
respected veteran, and seasoned programmer, was forced
into menial work until he retired in frustration. Others who
spoke up—like Fred Smith—were targeted and accused of
theft and misconduct. Fred was even arrested for allegedly
stealing a hard drive that Lewis himself had turned in
months earlier. Fred was humiliated, but later vindicated.
Lewis's abuse of power had no limits.

In time, I began hearing from coworkers — including people who were directly in that space every day — that Lewis had been the subject of serious complaints involving Andrea Marshall. I wasn't there, and I didn't see the paperwork, so I don't present any of it as fact. But what was shared with me was consistent: he was suddenly gone from the office for a period of time, and she was quietly moved soon after. Whether every detail was accurate or not, the reaction alone said enough. When concerns involved certain people, leadership acted swiftly and decisively. When concerns involved me — a disabled veteran simply asking for fairness — the standard changed completely. That contrast told me everything I needed to know about how selective accountability had become inside that building.

Transition Summary

As the months passed, it became clear that the promotion battles were never about paperwork or performance—they were about power and perception. The scars of favoritism ran deeper than any job title could heal. Yet, even in defeat, I carried a quiet conviction that justice would have its day.

But what I didn't know then was that the real test hadn't even begun. The promotions I lost would pale compared to what came next—the systematic stripping away of my position, my stability, and my peace of mind. What began as a fight for fairness would soon become a fight for survival.

In the chapters ahead, I'll show you how one denial after another became the spark that pushed me to the edge—and how I learned that even when they take everything from you, they can't take your purpose.

Chapter 5 – The Sin of Denial (Of the COVID Request)

Author's Reflection

when silence becomes a matter of survival. During the height of COVID-19, I realized that my silence could cost me my life. The same agency that claimed to protect veterans and their well-being had allowed one man—my supervisor, Bryant Lewis—to weaponize authority against compassion. He had every right to approve my reasonable accommodation request, and every reason to do so. Yet he chose denial. It was not a misunderstanding of policy; it was the deliberate act of someone who knew the risk and ignored it anyway.

The First Denial: CRSC Pay

Before any accommodation request or appeal, there was another denial—one that set the tone for everything that followed. My Combat-Related Special Compensation (CRSC) claim was rejected without reason that made sense. The program exists to offset the loss of retirement pay for service-connected disabilities caused by combat, yet somehow my service aboard a war craft delivering troops and ammunition during active operations didn't qualify.

I remember thinking, if this can be denied, what else can they take? That was the first time I felt the quiet cruelty of bureaucracy—when paperwork rewrote the truth of what I lived through. I had risked my life in combat zones, commanded men and materiel under fire, and carried those injuries home with me. Still, they found a way to call it 'non-qualifying.'

It wasn't just about money; it was about recognition. The denial wasn't the end of my fight—it was the beginning of a pattern. CRSC became the first line in a long record of institutional betrayal, each denial building on the last, until it became clear that truth alone was never enough.

When COVID swept across the nation, fear filled every hallway. The VA was supposed to be a refuge—a place that understood risk, illness, and sacrifice. For veterans like me, it was supposed to be a safe space. But inside that building, the virus wasn't the only thing spreading. So was arrogance, indifference, and the abuse of power.

When the pandemic began, every federal agency issued guidance for managers to protect employees with pre-existing conditions. I was one of those employees. My doctors had made it clear: exposure to COVID-19 could be deadly for me. My condition wasn't speculative—it was documented, chronic, and service-connected. I wasn't asking for luxury; I was asking for life. So I did what any responsible employee would do: I filed a formal request for reasonable accommodation to work safely.

That request landed on the desk of Bryant Lewis.

He had full authority to approve or deny it. There was no board, no committee, no appeal before the fact—just his decision. And that's what made it all the more sinister. He had the authority to save me, and he chose not to.

The guidance was clear: employees at high risk were to be offered telework or alternate duties. Other supervisors across the country were approving accommodations just like mine without hesitation. But Lewis wasn't like other supervisors. His actions weren't grounded in policy—they were driven by personal animus. To him, my vulnerability

wasn't a concern; it was an opportunity to assert control.
He denied my request outright, knowing full well what that
meant. It wasn't about work performance—it was about
power.

To this day, I can't shake the thought that he would have
rather seen me dead than succeed. That may sound harsh,
but it's the truth. You can't call it anything else when
someone knowingly places your life in harm's way after
being told exactly what's at stake.

I remember the denial letter like it was yesterday. Cold.
Clinical. Devoid of empathy. It didn't cite a lack of evidence
or an unmet requirement. It simply said no. No explanation,
no consideration, no follow-up. Just no. For a veteran who
had spent years serving this country, it was like a betrayal
written in black ink. The message was clear: you are
expendable.

I appealed. I made my case again, this time going above his
head. It wasn't out of defiance—it was desperation. When
you live with a service-connected disability, you understand
your limits better than anyone. I didn't want sympathy. I
wanted safety. When the upper management finally
reviewed my file, they were stunned. The accommodation
was legitimate. It met every single standard of approval.
There was no reason it should have been denied. And in
that moment, the inevitable truth was realized: he should
have never denied my request.

That revelation came too late to undo the emotional
damage. By then, I had spent weeks in fear, anxiety, and
frustration, wondering if each day walking into that
building could be the one that ended my life. The emotional
toll was as heavy as the risk itself. My trust in the system

was gone. The very agency meant to protect veterans had become the instrument of my potential destruction.

What made it worse was watching others receive approval overnight. Employees with far fewer risk factors were granted telework, reassignments, or flexible arrangements. I, a disabled combat veteran, was forced to report in person. Favoritism and retaliation had overtaken reason and fairness. I began to realize that Lewis's cruelty was deliberate— a culmination of years of resentment toward my perseverance and unwillingness to bend to his control.

There were nights I sat at home thinking about how close I was to the edge. I had served my country honorably. I had led men through conflict and delivered under pressure. And yet, my survival now depended on the mercy of a man who had long decided that mercy wasn't in his vocabulary.

When leadership finally corrected the mistake, I wasn't vindicated—I was exhausted. The damage had been done. The denial wasn't just a line of text—it was a message sent to every employee who watched it happen: that integrity didn't matter, and compassion was optional. The system had no safety net for moral failure.

But I refused to give up. I documented everything. I wrote every email, saved every denial, and made sure my truth would survive even if I didn't. Because for me, this wasn't about one request—it was about every veteran, every worker with a disability, and every person who ever trusted a system that failed them.

To those reading this who find themselves in the same position, remember this: standing up for your right to live safely is not rebellion—it's survival. There will always be people who mistake your courage for defiance, your requests for inconvenience. Let them. The truth is, your life matters more than their comfort. And when someone in authority chooses cruelty over compassion, their title may protect them for a time, but it cannot absolve them.

Bryant Lewis had the authority to deny my request—but authority without conscience is sin. And that's what this chapter is about. Not just a denial of paperwork, but the denial of humanity itself.

Chapter 6 – The Setup

Author's Reflection

Sometimes betrayal doesn't strike all at once — it builds quietly, like a fog settling over familiar ground. You don't see it until you're standing in the middle of it, wondering how people who once smiled in your face could plan your fall behind closed doors.

This is the story of the setup — not a single moment, but a carefully built path designed to make failure look self-inflicted.

The Shift in the Air

After my COVID accommodation request was denied, I could feel the air change. Meetings that once included me suddenly happened without me. Emails that used to flow freely now came through filtered or not at all. Tasks were reassigned quietly, just enough to create confusion — and confusion became ammunition.

No one said the word "target," but I could feel it. I wasn't being managed; I was being maneuvered.

Transfers and Retaliation

Before the final blow, I had been moved from one VA to another, each time told it was a fresh start. But the whisper traveled faster than I could. By the time I arrived, my reputation had already been escorted ahead of me by those determined to see me fail. Each transfer proved not renewal but repetition—a new stage for the same play.

The Trainer Turned Away

One of the most painful shifts came when the person assigned to train me — the one who initially understood my willingness to learn and adjust — suddenly withdrew.

Later, in testimony, that same trainer admitted he had been instructed to stop training me. That confession told me everything. The problem was never my ability; it was their agenda.

By cutting off my support, they could create the appearance of non-performance. The setup was simple: deny guidance, then penalize the outcome.

Counseling on False Grounds

The next stage was paperwork — the weapon of choice in bureaucratic warfare. A "counseling" memo appeared, alleging errors that originated from the very system I was prevented from accessing. It was written to look corrective but felt like documentation for an ending already decided.

I remember reading it and thinking, "If truth still matters, this will never stand." But truth had become negotiable. In an agency where perception outweighed proof, the record became the reality — and the record was being rewritten to erase me.

Isolation by Design

They called it "team adjustment," but what it really meant was isolation.

I was left out of project briefings, removed from email chains, and stripped of tools that once allowed me to work efficiently.

Every obstacle became a setup for another accusation: "Why wasn't this completed?"

Because I was never told it existed.

It's hard to fail at a job you're not allowed to perform — but that was the point.

The Role of Silence

What hurt most wasn't the paperwork or the whispers; it was the silence of those who knew.

People who had once confided in me now looked the other way. They knew what was happening — some had seen it before — but fear is a powerful gag order.

In government systems, silence keeps paychecks safe.

So, they watched a veteran being boxed out and buried under process, all while claiming to value integrity.

Retaliation Disguised as Procedure

When the setup was complete, retaliation didn't come as an outburst — it came dressed as policy.

Every move was cloaked in regulation, every blow softened with HR language. "We're just following procedure," they'd say.

But procedure isn't justice when it's weaponized.

They wanted the end result without the confrontation — a quiet removal, justified on paper, while those responsible kept their hands clean.

The Breaking Point

I reached a point where exhaustion met resolve. I realized that they weren't just trying to remove me from a job — they were trying to erase the narrative of what had really happened.

And that's when I started documenting everything: the missing emails, the conflicting instructions, the timeline of every denial.

I knew that if I didn't protect the truth, no one would.

Faith as Resistance

In the midst of their strategy, I found my own — faith.

Not passive faith, but the kind that fights quietly, records meticulously, and stands firm in the storm.

I prayed not for revenge but for revelation — that someday, everything hidden would come to light.

And as the setup unfolded, so did my clarity: this wasn't just about me. It was about every veteran, every employee, every person who had ever been silenced by a system that protects its own before it protects what's right.

Closing Reflection

The setup was never about my performance; it was about power.

They mistook my patience for weakness and my professionalism for permission.

But what they didn't understand is that veterans are built for adversity — trained to endure, to document, to adapt.

So even as they built a case against me, I was building a record against them.

And when the truth finally comes due, paper trails cut both ways.

Chapter 7 – The Fallout

After the Setup

The paperwork was finished, but the wreckage was just beginning. A system that should have corrected a mistake doubled down on it. What started as a false counseling session became an erasure plan executed with signatures and silence.

Management Knew

Some knew the truth before I was removed. Others learned afterward and did nothing. Their awareness should have triggered a reversal; instead, it cemented the lie. Each act of silence became complicity. When the people entrusted to uphold fairness knowingly let injustice stand, they turn process into cruelty.

The Conversation

The man who had once interviewed me—the same one who would later remove me—called me in. I told him plainly, "I don't want to lose my job. I can do this work." He looked almost amused. "Come on," he said. "You'll be all right. You get disability." A six-figure career, decades of service, and all the sacrifice behind it dismissed with a single shrug. He reduced my life's work to a check, as though military disability were a consolation prize for losing my livelihood.

Financial Freefall

When that door closed, every other one began to creak under the weight. Mortgages slipped behind, property taxes mounted, liens appeared like weeds. I didn't miss bills of this importance in my life, yet now I was juggling payments and choosing which utilities to keep on. The IRS doesn't wait for justice, and poverty doesn't pause for appeals.

What they took from me wasn't only income—it was stability, dignity, and control of my own narrative.

Collateral Damage

The fallout didn't stop with me. My family felt it first. I had always been the anchor—the one who could cover a someone's car payment, keep the lights on for a for family member or a mortgage teetering on foreclosure. I gave freely, never asking for repayment, only wanting to see my loved ones stay afloat. Then the day came when I couldn't help them anymore. I could barely help myself. Watching them struggle, knowing that if the system had done right by me they wouldn't be suffering, was its own kind of torment. They didn't just damage my career—they crippled the network of support that kept others safe.

Faith in the Ruins

I searched for meaning among the ruins. My faith became the one currency they couldn't devalue. I prayed not for revenge but for clarity, for proof that endurance still mattered. Somewhere deep inside, I knew this story had to be told—not to reopen wounds but to remind others that silence is not safety.

Closing Reflection

The setup ended on paper, but its echo reached every corner of my life. Yet even in loss, purpose began to whisper. The very people who thought they were burying me were, without knowing it, planting the seed for what would come next. Because when everything is stripped away, what remains is truth—and truth, once spoken, can't be undone.

Chapter 8 – The Chosen Ones

Power and Protection

In every system built on fear, there are always the chosen—

Not chosen for their courage, or their skill, or their merit,

but for their obedience.

The fallout from my removal revealed it all. The same names kept reappearing in promotions, in email chains, in awards for "excellence." It wasn't excellence being rewarded; it was alignment. They didn't have to be the best—just the safest. They had learned the unspoken rule: never question, never correct, never stand between leadership and the lie.

The Untouchables

There were those who could do no wrong, no matter how many wrongs they did. Their mistakes were quietly cleaned up, their absences excused, their missteps reframed as "learning opportunities."

Meanwhile, for people like me—those who asked questions, who wanted fairness—every detail became a weapon. A late email became a "pattern." A missing file became "neglect." The difference wasn't performance; it was privilege.

When the GS-12 realignment came, I watched others get their upgrades automatically—no paperwork, no waiting, no fight. For me, it was endless explanations, delays, and denials. The rules changed depending on who was standing in front of them.

I wasn't asking for special treatment. I was asking for equal treatment. And that, in their world, was an act of defiance.

Rewarded Silence

What I learned was simple but sickening: silence was currency.

Those who held their tongues got promoted. Those who spoke truth became "problems."

I saw individuals who participated in the very actions that harmed me rise into higher offices, their reputations spotless because they had mastered the art of pretending not to see.

Meanwhile, anyone who had tried to do what was right had been moved out, written up, or worn down.

They wanted obedience, not honesty. And they got it—at least for a while.

The Insider Network

By now, I knew how it worked.

If you were in the circle, mistakes disappeared.

If you were outside it, perfection wasn't enough.

The inner circle defended its own not through policy, but through quiet agreement. They traded favors, covered for each other's lapses, and made sure accountability stopped at the edge of their desks.

When it came to me, though, they found their backbone for discipline. Every standard suddenly mattered. Every comma, every clock tick, every technicality was magnified and used against me.

That wasn't leadership. That was control.

The Price of Principles

I didn't lose my job because I couldn't do it.

I lost it because I refused to play the game.

They wanted yes-men and echo chambers, not veterans who still believed in chain of command, accountability, and truth. The irony was unbearable—those of us trained to uphold integrity were punished by those who used integrity as a talking point.

They could have fixed what was wrong. Instead, they fixed the paperwork to make it look right.

The Hidden Meritocracy

Years later, I came to understand that I was never meant to be one of "the chosen."

My kind of loyalty—to truth, to veterans, to duty—doesn't fit neatly into their version of success.

But I wouldn't trade places with them. Their reward was comfort bought with silence. Mine was clarity bought with pain.

In a world that rewarded fear, I chose to stand for something. And though it cost me everything, I gained the one thing they'll never have: peace in knowing I didn't sell my soul for safety.

Transition

They chose themselves, and I chose truth.

And when the system pushed me out, I looked for another way to serve—

A way to rebuild, to keep moving forward, even when the doors of opportunity were slammed shut.

That search led me back to a place that was supposed to help veterans rebuild their futures: Vocational Rehabilitation.

Chapter 9 – The Voc Rehab Dilemma

I wish I could say the Voc Rehab denial surprised me, but by the time it arrived, I had already learned how this system treats the very people it claims to serve. Still, this one stung differently. VR&E wasn't about status. It wasn't about promotions. It wasn't even about recognition. It was about survival — the one program built specifically to help disabled veterans rebuild their lives and careers when the system has knocked them down.

I qualified under the Serious Employment Handicap (SEH) provision. Not just "technically." Not barely. I met the criteria exactly as written — the kind of case VR&E was created for. Recovering veterans who still want to work. Veterans trying to stay productive. Veterans trying to avoid the very path that leads to homelessness, hopelessness, or dependence. Veterans like me.

Yet instead of support, I received the same answer I had grown used to hearing: Denied.

What made this denial different was what it revealed. Up to that point, I kept telling myself maybe it was a misunderstanding… maybe someone overlooked a document… maybe I didn't explain something clearly. But VR&E wasn't confused — they were coordinated. This wasn't a clerical error or a training issue. They understood exactly what my plan was, and exactly why I qualified. And they shut the door anyway. Not with justification. Not with alternative solutions. Just a cold, bureaucratic "no," delivered without explanation or empathy.

It became the theme of that period of my life — every request that should have protected me, supported me, or given me a fair chance was dismissed as if my service meant nothing.

The Language of Denial

The thing about denials is that they don't come with honesty. They come dressed in polite phrases that hide the truth.

"Not recommended at this time."
"Your request cannot be accommodated."
"We have determined that you do not meet the criteria."

But behind those words is something much harsher:

We are choosing not to help you.
We are choosing not to support you.
We are choosing to look the other way.

They deny you — but they deny you softly, hoping the softness will keep you quiet.

I felt that same pattern when I requested telework during COVID. The federal guidance was clear: protect high-risk employees. I submitted my documentation. I wasn't asking for special treatment — just the protection that every high-risk employee was supposed to receive. Yet I was dismissed without cause, as if my health and safety were irrelevant.

The FOIA denial cut even deeper. I wasn't asking for secrets. I was asking for transparency — the records that shaped my demotion, my denied promotion, my entire fight to be treated fairly. Instead, they stonewalled, withheld, and delayed. FOIA exists to ensure accountability, but in reality, it became just another barrier. When an agency refuses to show you the rules they claim you violated, it tells you everything about the game you're trapped in.

And then there was the accommodation request. Every piece of medical evidence supported it. Other employees with comparable conditions had been granted the same accommodation without hesitation. Mine was denied, not because it lacked merit but because approving it would have meant admitting the truth — that their decisions had put me in harm's way.

Finally came the employment continuation. That denial wasn't about performance. It wasn't about conduct. It came after all the excuses had run out. When the system doesn't know what else to do with someone who stands up for themselves, it removes them. Not because they failed, but because they refused to stay silent.

A Pattern, Not a Mistake

As I sat with all of these denials — VR&E, COVID, FOIA, accommodation, telework, employment continuation — the truth finally settled in. These weren't isolated events. These weren't different offices making unrelated decisions. This was a pattern. A culture. A way of operating that punishes the veteran who pushes back, who asks questions, who demands fairness.

It wasn't that I was unqualified. It wasn't that I failed to follow procedure. It was that I refused to accept mistreatment quietly.

The denials were never about me being wrong — they were about me being inconvenient.

The Real Dilemma

The dilemma wasn't my VR&E plan. The dilemma was how a federal system built to support veterans could become the very thing that blocks them from rebuilding their lives.

I shouldn't have had to fight this hard.
I shouldn't have had to justify my worth to people who had the authority to help but chose not to.
I shouldn't have had to prove my disability, my struggle, or my potential over and over again.

But I did.

And somewhere between the VR&E denial and the refusal to let me continue working, I realized the truth: the system wasn't failing by accident. It was failing by design.

This chapter of my life wasn't about a single denial — it was about the slow, deliberate erosion of opportunity, dignity, and trust. And once I saw the pattern, I couldn't unsee it.

Chapter 9 marks the moment the story stopped being about paperwork and policies… and started being about the reality of how disabled veterans are treated when they become too informed, too outspoken, or too persistent.

This chapter wasn't the end of the fight. It was the beginning of understanding what I was truly up against.

Author's Reflection

When you stop asking why and start asking how. How did a system built to protect veterans become a maze that punishes them for trying to rise? For me, the answer came through a long line of closed doors — each stamped with the same word: Denied.

I had survived war, survived bureaucracy, and survived the isolation that comes when truth threatens comfort. But Voc Rehab was supposed to be different. It was supposed to be the path back — not just for me, but for every disabled veteran who still had fight left in them. Instead, it became the mirror reflecting everything broken in the system I once served.

Building with Purpose

When I applied for Vocational Rehabilitation and Employment, I wasn't chasing money. I was chasing meaning — a way to stay afloat while helping others do the same. Veteran Elite Services LLC was never about wealth; it was about service through self-reliance. I wanted to use my background in logistics and IT to create a company that hired and trained veterans, giving them the chance to rebuild with dignity instead of dependency.

I had the paperwork, the credentials, and a business plan rooted in accountability. Every expense justified, every goal measurable. If ever there were a blueprint for rehabilitation done right, this was it. But once again, initiative was treated like insubordination. Hope became suspect the moment it sounded confident.

From Encouragement to Evasion

At first, my counselor spoke in promises — "We'll explore the self-employment track." "This looks promising." But that tone shifted once my proposal reached the upper chain. The encouragement faded into delay. Delay turned into avoidance. And avoidance became the quiet weapon of denial.

They told me my plan was "too ambitious," as if veterans weren't allowed to dream beyond survival. They told me my costs were "unnecessary," even though every item was tied to productivity and compliance. They said I should "look for employment instead" — as if self-employment weren't employment at all. The irony burned: a system designed to help veterans regain control of their lives couldn't handle one who already had a plan.

Faith Without Favor

I kept reminding myself that faith had carried me through worse. But it was hard not to notice a pattern forming. Every request I made — every attempt to assert my rights, my safety, or my vision — hit the same wall. And over time, those denials began to look less like isolated decisions and more like chapters of one long campaign to wear me down.

The Pattern Revealed

What this taught me was simple: it was never about paperwork. It was about power — who gets to wield it, who dares to question it, and who pays the price for doing so. When a veteran asks for fairness, the system sees a threat; when he builds his own path, they call it arrogance. They can't fathom that sometimes strength comes not from defiance, but from faith. And faith, unlike funding, cannot be denied.

Closing Reflection

Systemic Silence and the Illusion of Support

What made it worse wasn't just the denials — it was the silence that followed them. I reached out to every organization that claimed to help veterans: call centers, advocacy offices, online portals, even congressional liaisons. What I got back was delay, confusion, or nothing at all.

Messages went unanswered. Numbers disconnected. Websites promised connection but led to dead ends. Every link seemed to break right when help was supposed to begin. It was as if the system had been designed to exhaust you into giving up.

Veterans shouldn't need a master's degree in bureaucracy to get basic assistance. For me, it was like dialing 911 during an emergency and getting a busy signal. That's what it felt like — an emergency without responders.

If the nation can send soldiers into war with full coordination, it should be able to coordinate care when those same soldiers come home broken and need help. If that means hiring more people, then hire more people. If that means creating a true repository — a one-stop point of contact where veterans can get immediate attention instead of being passed in circles — then build it.

The current structure rewards delay, not duty. And for every unanswered call or unreturned email, another veteran slips deeper into despair. We deserve a system that answers when we call, not one that pretends the silence is service.

So I moved forward in faith — still waiting, still believing — carrying the same strength that got me through war and through Washington. Because even without approval, the mission doesn't stop; purpose doesn't need permission.

Chapter 10 – A Call to Accountability

There comes a point when silence is no longer survival —
it's surrender. For years, veterans have been told to be
patient, to wait for the system to work itself out, to file
another form and hope for fairness. But patience has
become the shield behind which neglect hides.
Accountability is not vengeance; it is the only path to
restoration.

The Moral Debt

When a nation sends men and women to serve, it incurs a
lifelong moral debt — a promise written not on paper but in
blood and sacrifice. That promise was captured in Abraham
Lincoln's timeless charge: "to care for him who shall have
borne the battle, and for his widow, and his orphan." Those
words were not poetic; they were policy. They were the
standard by which America agreed to measure its own soul.
Yet today that promise is fractured. Bureaucracy has
replaced compassion. Procedure has replaced purpose. And
somewhere between the paperwork and the politics, the
humanity has been lost.

Systemic Neglect

The failures described in these pages are not the story of
one department, one decision, or one individual. They form
a pattern — a structure built to protect the institution
rather than the people it serves. Policies meant to safeguard
fairness have become shields against accountability.
Whistleblowers are silenced. Records are buried under
layers of process. Decisions that harm are defended as
"policy-compliant." And when veterans cry out, they are met
not with empathy but with audits, investigations, and
silence.

Accountability means more than identifying what went
wrong. It requires confronting why it keeps happening —

the culture of self-preservation that punishes truth and rewards compliance. The same system that failed one veteran will fail another unless it is rebuilt on transparency and trust.

The Ripple Effect
Every act of institutional neglect ripples outward. It weakens families, erodes faith in government, and feeds the quiet despair of those who once believed their service mattered. A nation cannot call itself strong when those who defended it must fight another war just to be heard. The struggle for justice is not a personal grievance; it is a national mirror reflecting who we have become and what we are willing to ignore.

The Higher Standard
True accountability begins with courage — the courage to admit wrong, to release hidden truths, and to rebuild systems that serve people first. It requires leadership that values integrity over image, and oversight that sees veterans not as statistics but as citizens whose service earned more than lip service.

If Lincoln's words are to mean anything in the modern era, they must be reclaimed as a living oath: "To care for those who have borne the battle — not selectively, not conditionally, but completely."

A Nation's Test
History will remember not only how veterans fought abroad but how their country treated them at home. The measure of a government is not in its speeches but in its stewardship of trust. That trust has been broken — yet it can still be repaired. But repair demands action: policy reform, cultural change, and the moral will to ensure that no veteran ever faces institutional betrayal again.

Chapter 11 – The Follow-Up

They count on you to stop asking. That's the unspoken strategy buried deep within the system — the quiet hope that time, fatigue, and frustration will finish the job that policy began. But I never stopped. I followed up, because silence is not an answer, and delay is not a defense.

The Waiting Game
Every request seemed to vanish into a void labeled 'in review.' Weeks became months, months became years. Forms were returned for missing commas, emails acknowledged but never answered. The bureaucracy knew how to stall without ever saying no. For veterans, waiting became a second deployment — one fought in inboxes and call queues instead of combat zones.

Building the Record
Every follow-up was a form of testimony. I kept the confirmations, the ticket numbers, the 'please be patient' replies. They weren't just receipts — they were proof that the system knew and still did nothing. Following up wasn't persistence; it was survival. The trail of unanswered correspondence became the evidence of neglect itself.

When Silence Becomes Policy
It's one thing to make a mistake; it's another to make non-response the standard. In every agency I reached out to — from VA divisions to oversight offices — the pattern repeated. No one owned the failure. Each department pointed to another. The result was paralysis disguised as procedure. Accountability died not from hostility but from indifference.

Retaliation Always Has Footprints

If there is one thing I learned through this entire process, it is that retaliation doesn't come with a warning label. It doesn't show up with a signature or a confession. It shows up in patterns — sudden hostility, coordinated narratives, and convenient accusations that appear only after you speak up.

That's exactly what happened after I filed my EEOC complaint.

Almost overnight, people who had never expressed a single concern about me suddenly produced handwritten statements describing a "hostile work environment." Calvin Williams — a man who had spoken to me respectfully for years — submitted a letter claiming he felt unsafe and intimidated. Andrea Marshall submitted one as well. Neither accusation reflected reality, and both appeared only after leadership needed a way to discredit me.

I don't blame them. I know how that environment worked. When someone in power wanted a narrative created, people complied to avoid becoming the next target. Inside those walls, silence was survival and agreement was protection. I saw it happen to others long before it was aimed at me.

But the timing spoke louder than their words ever could. For years, no complaints. Then — the moment I filed EEOC — suddenly I was a threat. Suddenly I was dangerous. Suddenly the story had to shift. The letters weren't reflections of my character; they were reflections of a system doing whatever it could to bury the truth and protect itself.

Anyone who has ever filed a complaint against power knows this pattern. They don't address your claim — they attack your credibility. They don't fix the problem — they redefine you as the problem. That was the playbook. And it was executed with precision.

What they didn't realize was that every one of those letters only strengthened my resolve. If they had truly believed their accusations, they would have raised concerns long before. The fact that everything appeared *after* I took action told me everything I needed to know. Retaliation isn't always loud — sometimes it shows up on official letterhead, signed by people who were pressured to participate.

I carried the weight of those lies for a long time. Not because I feared them, but because they distorted the truth of who I was as a leader, a veteran, and a man. Writing this book finally gives me the chance to set the record right — not out of bitterness, but out of clarity. Truth deserves daylight, even when systems try to hide it.

Through it all, I stayed grounded in who I was. I remembered what my mother taught me back in Columbus, Mississippi—to stand firm in truth and keep faith no matter how dark it gets. So I kept working, documenting everything, and fighting to be treated with the same respect I had given others. I didn't fight out of anger; I fought out of purpose—because I knew that one day my story would be told, not just for me, but for every veteran, every worker, and every person silenced by fear of retaliation.

If you are reading this and find yourself in the same kind of storm—hold steady. You will be tested, isolated, and misunderstood. But truth has a long memory. You may lose position, but never lose your integrity. When I lost my job, I didn't lose myself. I walked away with my head high, knowing that every act of courage writes its own legacy. The system may try to erase your contributions, but God's record never loses track.

The Emotional Toll
You start to question whether your time, your service, or even your voice still matter. Every day without an answer chips away at dignity. For some veterans, that silence becomes too heavy to carry. It's not the denial that breaks you — it's the waiting that never ends.

Turning Follow-Up into Reform
Following up taught me that policy change begins with persistence. What if every agency had to log unanswered inquiries publicly? What if delays were tracked like performance metrics? What if silence itself triggered oversight? We can build a system that measures responsiveness as seriously as it measures compliance.

The Next Chapter Isn't Written Yet
The follow-up continues — in letters, appeals, and accountability. Because asking again isn't pestering; it's proof that truth still matters. And if the system ever learns to answer without being cornered, maybe then we'll finally have justice worthy of those who served.

NO MORE VETERAN CLAIM BACKLOG = A REAL MISSION

There are moments when this country moves fast: money
gets allocated, thousands of people get hired, temporary
programs get launched, and massive problems get
addressed almost overnight. We have seen it during natural
disasters, public health emergencies, economic bailouts,
and immigration operations. That proves one thing — when
America decides something is urgent, it knows how to
move.

Veterans make up a small fraction of the population. There
are roughly 15–18 million living veterans, and a little over
one hundred thousand backlogged claims. Compared to
other national challenges, that number is manageable —
unbelievably manageable. Which raises the question: why
hasn't there been a focused effort to eliminate it?

A realistic plan would be a Veterans Claims Surge Corps —
a temporary, trained workforce whose only job is to clear
the backlog. No distractions, no endless meetings, no
bureaucracy — just processing claims and appeals with
accuracy and fairness.

Who could serve on this team?
- Retired VA raters
- Former military personnel with admin/legal experience
- Retired federal or GS-level employees with claim
familiarity
- Contracted claims specialists already versed in VA
procedures

They would be trained once, assigned one mission, and
their work would sunset after that mission is complete. Not

another permanent agency — but a time-limited strike force.

A simple three-lane triage system could open the logjam immediately:
Fast Lane: Terminal illness, homeless veterans, elderly claims
Standard Lane: New or recent claims needing full review
Consolidation Lane: Multiple claims from the same vet — to prevent duplication and confusion

Technology could assist with collecting documents and flagging missing evidence — but final decisions should remain human. A veteran should never be denied because a document was missing that the VA itself should have requested.

If America can move entire operations for other national issues, then fixing the veteran backlog is not impossible — it has simply never been treated as urgent. We do not need a new department. We need a one-time national surge, staffed by people who understand the system and are willing to finish what has been left undone.

Veterans do not need slogans. They need decisions.
They do not need new committees. They need action.
And they do not need another policy phrase.
They need people hired, trained, and assigned one mission — finish the job, and do it right.

This could be done. Not someday — now.

WHY THIS STORY MATTERS — BEYOND THE VETERAN

Some may believe this journey is only about veterans —
that it begins and ends with uniforms and service.
But that isn't true.

When a veteran is affected, a family is affected.
A spouse feels the strain.
Children notice the silence.
Parents witness their hero carry invisible weight.
Brothers and sisters wait for words they can't always find.

So when we protect veterans —
we are protecting the homes they return to.
The people who believed in them.
The generations that follow after.

This story is not only about those who served —
it is about those who stayed, waited, supported, and
prayed.

You cannot lift a veteran
without lifting their family.

That is why this fight matters —
because veterans do not stand alone,
and neither should the people who love them.

From Encouragement to Evasion

At first, my counselor spoke in promises — "We'll explore the self-employment track." "This looks promising." But that tone shifted once my proposal reached the upper chain. The encouragement faded into delay. Delay turned into avoidance. And avoidance became the quiet weapon of denial.

They told me my plan was "too ambitious," as if veterans weren't allowed to dream beyond survival. They told me my costs were "unnecessary," even though every item was tied to productivity and compliance. They said I should "look for employment instead" — as if self-employment weren't employment at all. The irony burned: a system designed to help veterans regain control of their lives couldn't handle one who already had a plan.

Faith Without Favor

I kept reminding myself that faith had carried me through worse. But it was hard not to notice a pattern forming. Every request I made — every attempt to assert my rights, my safety, or my vision — hit the same wall. And over time, those denials began to look less like isolated decisions and more like chapters of one long campaign to wear me down.

The Pattern Revealed

What this taught me was simple: it was never about paperwork. It was about power — who gets to wield it, who dares to question it, and who pays the price for doing so. When a veteran asks for fairness, the system sees a threat; when he builds his own path, they call it arrogance. They can't fathom that sometimes strength comes not from defiance, but from faith. And faith, unlike funding, cannot be denied.

Closing Reflection

Systemic Silence and the Illusion of Support

What made it worse wasn't just the denials — it was the silence that followed them. I reached out to every organization that claimed to help veterans: call centers, advocacy offices, online portals, even congressional liaisons. What I got back was delay, confusion, or nothing at all.

Messages went unanswered. Numbers disconnected. Websites promised connection but led to dead ends. Every link seemed to break right when help was supposed to begin. It was as if the system had been designed to exhaust you into giving up.

Veterans shouldn't need a master's degree in bureaucracy to get basic assistance. For me, it was like dialing 911 during an emergency and getting a busy signal. That's what it felt like — an emergency without responders.

If the nation can send soldiers into war with full coordination, it should be able to coordinate care when those same soldiers come home broken and need help. If that means hiring more people, then hire more people. If that means creating a true repository — a one-stop point of contact where veterans can get immediate attention instead of being passed in circles — then build it.

The current structure rewards delay, not duty. And for every unanswered call or unreturned email, another veteran slips deeper into despair. We deserve a system that answers when we call, not one that pretends the silence is service.

So I moved forward in faith — still waiting, still believing —
carrying the same strength that got me through war and
through Washington. Because even without approval, the
mission doesn't stop; purpose doesn't need permission.

Final Word

When I look back on everything I endured — the denials, the dismissals, the setbacks, the retaliation — I no longer see a story about paperwork or policies. I see a story about a system that asks everything of its veterans, but too often gives nothing back when we need it most. I see the cost of silence, the price of speaking up, and the weight carried by anyone who refuses to bow to injustice.

But I also see something else: I'm still here.
I'm still standing.
I'm still telling the truth.

This book isn't just about what happened to me. It's about what happens to veterans across this country every single day — those who try to follow the rules, those who try to rebuild their lives, those who knock on the door of the very institution that promised to support them, only to be turned away. My story is just one example of what so many endure quietly, privately, without the resources or voice to fight back.

If you take anything from these pages, let it be this: **your struggle is not a personal failure.** The challenges you face are not because you lacked effort, intelligence, or discipline. Many times, the system itself creates barriers that no one should have to climb alone. And when the system fails, the veteran is left to pick up the pieces — emotionally, financially, physically — while still carrying the weight of service.

Yet even in the face of that reality, I believe in something bigger than the institutions that let us down. I believe in the strength of veterans. I believe in the communities that surround us. I believe in the power of telling the truth, even when it costs us something. Especially when it costs us something.

If you are a veteran reading this, know that you are not invisible. You are not forgotten. And you are not alone in your fight. If you are a family member, friend, or advocate, know that your support matters more than you will ever realize. And if you work in the system — if you are part of the structure that holds veteran lives in its hands — I hope this book encourages reflection, compassion, and a commitment to doing better.

My journey isn't over. But telling this story is a step toward reclaiming what was taken from me and refusing to let the truth be buried under bureaucracy. It is my reminder — to myself and to others — that resilience doesn't come from being unbroken. It comes from rising after being knocked down.

And as long as I have breath, I'm going to keep rising.

FINAL SALUTE

This toast began more than forty years ago during my early days in the Navy. There was no script, no handbook, no Facebook, and no one to follow. It was just me and my shipmates — DeBerry, Chambers, Rivers, Finch, and others who can attest to the toast's originality — trading lines back and forth until the words found their shape. We didn't borrow it from anyone — it came from our own time, our own minds, and our own voices. We spoke it into existence, and it stayed with us ever since.

I won't debate where it may have traveled afterward — but I know where it started, and I know how it shaped me. How fitting — how ironic — and how valid it is that something formed in a moment of fatigue, laughter, and survival would end up following me across decades of struggle and perseverance. It wasn't just a toast. It became part of my life — a mindset, a backbone, and a quiet reminder that we endured what others might not even understand.

This is that original toast.

Up to it, down to it,
F**k those that can't do it,
We do it, because we're used to it.
GET SOME.

It started with just a few of us — but in my story, it became something bigger. It became proof of where I came from…
and how I'm still standing.

This photograph on the next page is more than four decades old now — faded at the edges, a little grainy, softened by time. But even with the years worn into it, the truth it captures is unmistakable. I'm the young sailor on the far left, barely eighteen, standing with shipmates who were still becoming family. None of us understood at that moment how much those early days would shape us, or how the simple things — camaraderie, grit, and humor — would carry us through the hardest parts of our lives.

If you look closely at the man pointing in front, you can just make out the original toast embroidered across the back of his shirt. It's faint now, but it's real — a small, almost hidden detail that says everything about where this story began. Before the decades. Before the battles. Before any of us knew what life would demand from us.

This picture isn't polished or posed. It wasn't meant to be symbolic. But today, it stands as a reminder that even the rough, imperfect moments can leave a lasting mark. The years have changed us all, but the foundation we built back then — the pride, the resilience, the unspoken brotherhood — remains as solid as ever. And it's from that foundation that I continue to rise.

Photo courtesy of Timothy Rivers